Journeying in Joy and Gladness

Lent & Holy Week
with
Gaudete et Exsultate

Kevin O'Gorman SMA

First published in 2019 by Messenger Publications

Cover image: Zamurovic Photography / Shutterstock

ISBN 978 1 78812 0180

Designed by Messenger Publications Design Department
Cover Image © Thoom / Shutterstock
Typeset in Baskerville & Amrigo
Printed by Nicholson & Bass Ltd

Messenger Publications,
37 Lower Leeson Street, Dublin D02 W938
www.messenger.ie

Abbreviated Titles:
Gaudete et Exsultate, 'Rejoice and Be Glad' (GE)
Evangelii Gaudium, 'The Joy of the Gospel' (EG)
Evangelii Nuntiandi, 'Evangelisation in the Modern World' (EN)
Amoris Laetitia, 'The Joy of Love' (AL)
Gaudium et Spes, 'Joy and Hope' (GS)

ASH WEDNESDAY

The Lord asks everything of us, and in return he offers us true life, the happiness for which we were created (GE, 1)

Lent does not normally begin with happiness. We are more accustomed to hearing of how hard it will be. The theme of conversion, which the season of Lent begins with, is often understood in terms of sacrifice, struggle and even suffering. An overly moralistic approach to Lent means, however, that Christians can sometimes look, in a line from the Pope's previous Exhortation *Evangelii Gaudium* (The Joy of the Gospel), 'like someone who has just come back from a funeral' (EG, 10). The challenge of the Gospel is to consider the call to repentance in the light of what we receive from God. This means holding the darkness of our lives up against the light of God's love, seeing the contrast between the sin of the world and the salvation offered in the kingdom of God.

Pope Francis is clear that Lenten and lifelong conversion 'asks everything of us'. Conversion asks for change in mind, heart and even body, perhaps even to the extent of losing our lives. However, Pope Francis is equally clear that conversion will not cost happiness, will not cheat us of human fulfilment. Happiness hinges on holiness. True human happiness needs the healing and hope that holiness holds out; holiness helps us become fully human. Offering everything is not one option among others but an opening of our minds, hearts and bodies to truth, love and wholeness. The goal of conversion is communion with God and others. Repentance is a turning towards holiness, returning to receive 'the happiness for which we were created'. Holiness is the hallmark of authentic happiness.

THURSDAY AFTER ASH WEDNESDAY

For the Lord has chosen each one of us 'to be holy and blameless before him in love' (Eph 1:4) (GE, 1)

Wherever we head on land, sea or sky we encounter a horizon. This is due to the curvature of the earth. Horizons hold a sense of limitation, of boundary and being hedged in. Showing a slice of space (and time) a horizon serves as a metaphor for the human condition, calling to mind the contingency of life and reminding us of our mortality. At the same time horizons are beacons of hope, beckoning us beyond the confines of the present towards the possibilities of the future. As the proverb reminds us, faraway hills are forever green. Encounter and horizon are two favourite images of Pope Francis. For him encounter expresses an engagement with others that is ethical because of the Gospel. This is encounter as evangelisation. The experience of God's love exhorts and energises us to go out of ourselves and give to others. Horizon describes the direction in which we are drawn – more and more towards holiness. A holiness that the Second Vatican Council teaches is the perfection of love. Love leads to holiness and holiness is lived out in love.

The call to conversion at the beginning of Lent is an invitation to look at our lives and ask whether they are oriented towards the holiness and goodness that are at the heart of love. In stating that each person is chosen 'to be holy and blameless before him in love' Francis is speaking of the need to look closely at our lives and lifestyles. Lent is not the issuing of a list of dos and don'ts but an invitation to love. This is not a human resources exercise where boxes are ticked off in an inventory of the moral and even spiritual life. Instead it involves looking at the mindset and listening to the heart that guides our lifestyle, to consider and choose what brings us blamelessness and blessedness rather than bitterness and banishment.

FRIDAY AFTER ASH WEDNESDAY

All the faithful are called by the Lord – each in their own way – to that perfect holiness by which the Father himself is perfect (GE, 10)

This quote, taken from the Second Vatican Council's document on the Church, provides Pope Francis with the blueprint to lay out the path to holiness. This path involves a personal journey undertaken with the support of the saints, past and present, those named and unnamed, whom he calls the saints 'next door'. While conversion is ultimately personal we are reminded that 'no one is saved alone, as an isolated individual' (Interview with Pope Francis, Fr Antonio Spadaro, 2013). Conversion is the experience of salvation, conferred in the company of the saints and celebrated in the community of the Church.

The personal journey to holiness creates a path in the course of life which is unique, particular to the circumstances in which any person makes choices and lives or – in the case of martyrdom – dies by their consequences. This cannot be programmed in advance. Examples from the lives of the saints cannot be employed in a 'cut and paste' fashion as Pope Francis warns, adverting to St John of the Cross who 'preferred to avoid hard and fast rules for all' (GE, 11). In his existential and expressive style Francis states that 'the important thing is that each believer discern his or her own path, that they bring out the very best of themselves, rather than hopelessly trying to imitate something not meant for them' (GE, 11). Conversion is certainly not a competition with others for the crown of holiness. The call to holiness is to find in faith, follow in love and forge in hope 'the one specific path that the Lord has in mind for us'. Francis's words of encouragement are a celebration of the journey made by 'each in their own way' (GE, 10) as a personal contribution to the communion of saints. Only in this way can we become 'fully mature with the fullness of Christ himself' (Eph 4:13) and come to the perfection through the Holy Spirit to which the Father calls us all.

SATURDAY AFTER ASH WEDNESDAY

We are all called to be holy by living our lives with love and by bearing witness in everything we do, wherever we find ourselves (GE, 14)

Francis follows his proclamation of the personal vocation to holiness with the principle of love and witness that applies to all Christians, 'wherever we find ourselves'. This approach affords him the opportunity to give a number of examples. The life of someone called and committed to the consecrated life in the Church is to be shown by a spirit of joy, exhibiting an enthusiasm for evangelisation, while the mission of the married is to take care of each other as they share in and strive to show Christ's love for the Church. In the style of John the Baptist he tells those who work for a living to conduct themselves conscientiously and competently in contributing to the welfare of others. Parents and godparents are exhorted to become holy 'by patiently teaching the little ones to follow Jesus' (GE, 14), while people in authority are expected to forego personal gain for the common good.

This encouragement of people to sanctity with examples from different states and situations in life echoes the words of Pope St Paul VI in *Evangelii Nuntiandi* about the primacy of proclaiming the Gospel by witnesses who, especially, through their 'wordless witness' stir up irresistible questions in the hearts of those who see how they live: Why are they like this? Why do they live in this way? What or who is it that inspires them? Why are they in our midst?' (EN, 21) The phrase 'caught not taught' pertains to holiness as much – if indeed not more so – as any other part of people's experience. Holiness is not the icing on the cake, added on at the end. This is the message of Francis's exhortation to be 'witnesses in everything we do'.

FIRST WEEK

SUNDAY

At its core, holiness is experiencing, in union with Christ, the mysteries of his life (GE, 20)

In a memorable phrase the Second Vatican Council described a Christian 'as one who has been made a partner in the paschal mystery'. The call to holiness is to make this partnership as personally complete as possible through that conversion which Pope Francis says 'consists in uniting ourselves to the Lord's death and resurrection in a unique way, constantly dying and rising with him'. Spelling out what 'in a unique way' means, Francis mentions that sharing in the paschal mystery can involve identifying with a particular part or period of the earthly life of Jesus which is the prelude to his passion and resurrection. The temptations that Jesus endured, expressed in this Gospel reading, offer an invaluable entry point for contemplating, both personally and communally, how to respond to the invitation to imitate Jesus.

The three temptations in turn entice Jesus to become an exhibitionist, build an earthly empire or be an exclusive egoist. The exhibitionist aims for the spectacular event to show off and be seen as victorious and not a victim. Not satisfied with surprise and scorning simplicity for the spectacular, the exhibitionist may employ means that are shocking and even violent. The empire builder seeks superior status by showing a superfluity of power and privilege, pleasure and possessions or some sum of these. Prepared to sacrifice everything in the blind pursuit of these, the sacrifice of others for this end is simply seen as part of the price to be paid for personal gain and grandiosity. Unlike the exhibitionist and empire builder, the egoist has no need for applause or accumulation, acting out of arrogance and the ambition to be absolutely self-determining. Focusing on the exhibitionist's envy, the emperor's gluttony and the egoist's pride, this first Sunday in Lent furnishes a lens for looking at one's moral and spiritual stance to see if it shares in and shows the mysteries of Christ's life.

MONDAY

Holiness is nothing other than charity lived to the full (GE, 21)

This line, taken from Pope Francis's predecessor, recalls the three forms of love reflected on by Pope Emeritus Benedict XVI in his encyclical *Deus caritas est* – God is love (2005): *eros*, *philia* and *agape*. While the first two, romantic love and love of friendship were well known to people living and writing before Christ, the third features the love found only in Christ. As Pope Francis states, 'In the end, it is Christ who loves in us' (GE, 21). Christ can love in and through us because he has first loved us, as St John says, 'to the end' (Jn 13:1). He is not merely a model but the medium of God's mercy, an exemplar who enables us to imitate the ideal of love without limits. Holiness is love lived to the full.

Lent invites us to let the love of God in Christ lay a foundation within and among us, forming attitudes and actions founded on grace. Only in this way can we stop weighing charity and worrying about what we can afford to commit ourselves to. Charity is not contributing or, worse still, conceding the leftovers of our lives, counted out after we have first taken care of ourselves and those close to us. Like mercy, it cannot be measured. Charity is not one value among others that can come into conflict depending on the circumstances. It is a vision that lays claim to the lot rather than to little bits here and there. Worrying about being charitable is a contradiction in terms because it betrays a lack of freedom to live love to the full. The currency of charity is generosity, captured in the words of St Ignatius of Loyola, 'to give and not to count the cost save that of doing God's most holy will'. God's will is that we should become holy in Christ, witnessed in living love to the full.

TUESDAY

Allow the Spirit to forge in you the personal mystery that can reflect Jesus Christ in today's world (GE, 23)

Four words are essential for Pope Francis and fortunately each begins with 'e': evangelisation, encounter, example and encouragement. His encouragement is wonderfully formulated and felt in paragraphs 22–24 of *Gaudete*. After expressing that not everything a saint has said or done in the course of their life is necessarily laudable, he emphasises that we need to look at the whole, 'their entire journey of growth in holiness' (GE, 22) which enables us to 'grasp their overall meaning as a person' (GE, 22). We are encouraged to take this trajectory and apply it to our own journey.

Every Christian enjoys a call, paraphrasing St Thérèse of Lisieux, to be holiness at the heart of the Church. This is a 'powerful summons to all of us' (GE, 23) that both respects and regards the experience of each person who seeks the inspiration of the Holy Spirit in the interior movements that make up the story of their life. No moment or matter is excluded from this sense of mission. Like the facets of a diamond in the sunlight, the action of the Spirit is to illuminate each aspect of a person's pathway through life, integrating all into a unique pattern of perfection. By fusing mission with mystery in the meaning of a person's vocation to holiness, Francis is reminding all members of the Church that they must see themselves foremost as missionaries. Dovetailing the dignity and demands of discipleship requires discernment, discovering through prayer and the signs of the Spirit how each decision and deed can disclose the presence and power of Christ. In a final and felicitious note of encouragement Francis says that failures in the course of a particular mission are not fatal, for 'the Lord will bring it to fulfilment despite your mistakes and missteps' (GE, 24) as long as a person continues to relate lovingly and remains open to the grace of God which heals, holding out hope for the rest of the journey.

WEDNESDAY

Just as you cannot understand Christ apart from the kingdom he came to bring, so too your personal mission is inseparable from the building of that kingdom (GE, 25)

In Mark's Gospel Jesus' call to repentance comes after his revelation of the Reign of God: 'The time is fulfilled, and the kingdom of God has come near' (Mk 1:15). The Reign of God is the central reference point for the preaching and practice of Jesus. The purpose of his mission was to make known the kingdom of his heavenly Father. This is a kingdom of mercy not mastery, compassion not control, communion not conflict. In his ministry Jesus presented this vision through his message and miracles, by his words and works. Having once spoken about the need for a seed to die, ultimately Jesus was prepared to lay down his life for the sake of the kingdom of God, leaving it to his Father to bring it about through his resurrection. Inseparable from his mission, the kingdom is the meaning of Jesus' own identity as Son of God, to the extent that Origen once called him 'the kingdom-in-person'.

Francis says that our 'identification with Christ and his will involves a commitment to build with him that kingdom of love, justice and universal peace' (GE, 25). Invited ourselves to inhabit the kingdom of God, we are called to help insert it in the world through our own integrity and interaction with others in terms of the gospel values of love, justice and peace. Lent asks us to look on these values as part of the vocation to a 'personal mission' with a view to see how we can play our part to incarnate them in the particular circumstances of the human condition we find ourselves in. While indicating the dignity of being blessed to belong with Christ to the kingdom of God, Francis insists that we do our individual best to bring about its values for the peoples and places in the world we are born into and become a part of.

THURSDAY

It is not healthy to love silence while fleeing interaction with others, to want peace and quiet while avoiding activity, to seek prayer while disdaining service (GE, 26)

From the outset of his papacy Francis has proclaimed that spirituality does not separate Christians from concern for the world or shut them off from encounter and engagement with others. The call to holiness is not an escape clause from the human condition, exempting the search for sanctity from a sense of solidarity with people and their struggles. It is not surprising that, as a Jesuit, he should quote the central Ignatian insight, 'we are called to be contemplatives even in the midst of action' (GE, 26). The 'even' here is not a concession but a condition, a challenge to be conscious of the capacity to cultivate contemplation in the course of action.

The hinge here is the connection between healthy and holy. Holiness does not bypass what is humanly healthy, both psychologically and physically, socially and culturally. As St Thomas Aquinas famously formulated, grace presupposes nature and perfects it. Prayer is not a trap door through which we flee from the world with its warts, wounds and worries. The desire for prayer does not disdain the spirit of service. This truth is seen in the three legs of Lent, linking prayer with fasting and almsgiving. Contemplation does not cut out charity and care for the environment. As Christians we are not called to isolate ourselves but to become involved with others which means that 'everything can be accepted and integrated into our life in this world and become a part of our path to holiness' (GE, 26). From the sanctuary we are sent forth in mission, mindful that faith leads us to find God in all things.

FRIDAY

We are challenged to show our commitment in such a way that everything we do has evangelical meaning and identifies us all the more with Jesus Christ (GE, 28)

Peter could justifiably be considered the patron saint of Lent. Throughout this liturgical season he is seen continually side by side with Jesus. With James and John he treks up Mount Tabor to catch a glimpse of the glory of Jesus. Travelling to Jerusalem he is present at all events leading up to the Last Supper and witnesses some of the scene of Jesus' agony in Gethsemane despite his weariness. His arrogant boast of standing with his Master even to the bloody end is brought to a bitter denouement when he denies Jesus and breaks down in tears of total regret. Despite his personal frailty and public failure, Peter's human story is a continual reminder of the honesty, humility and hope that are at the heart of conversion.

Happily his failure is not the sum of his story. As the disciple who asked his Master how many times he must forgive his brother who has sinned against him, Peter experiences the forgiveness of the Risen Lord at Easter and is enabled to follow Jesus fully, becoming in his ministry more and more conformed to the Christ he once confessed and later denied. Perhaps more properly and profitably he should be called the patron saint of Lent leading to Easter. Personally challenged to learn that everything in his personal mission 'has evangelical meaning' (GE, 28), he becomes leader by identifying himself 'all the more with Jesus Christ' (GE, 28). In this way, by his witness and even weakness, he is the fisherman who became the first Pope, providing the prime example of the pathway to holiness that his successor Francis proposes.

SATURDAY

This does not mean ignoring the need for moments of quiet, solitude and silence before God. Quite the contrary. The presence of constantly new gadgets, the excitement of travel and an endless array of consumer goods at times leaves no room for God's voice to be heard (GE, 29)

Francis here identifies three temptations for today's world, each of them beginning with the letter 't': technology, travel and things. The advent of the digital age, with access to information that is being continually uploaded, has augmented rather than alleviated anxiety. A 'touch of a button' ethos has become almost absolute with apps available for most areas of life. Space for reflection and contemplation is in constant danger of becoming smaller in the digital universe. While traditionally travel was taught in terms of broadening the mind, today it may be thought of as a testimony to restlessness and to a lack of rootedness in both place and a shared perspective on life. Consumerism creates or at least contributes to what Francis calls elsewhere a 'throwaway culture' where people are thought of and treated as commodities.

At the heart of the temptation to excessive reliance on technology is the question of time. How we use our time both in labour and leisure is at the core of the Lenten call to conversion. To lessen the grip of gadgets, going and goods on our lives leaves time for 'quiet, solitude and silence before God'. To take time for the things of God that are our true treasure is the antidote to the anxiety and anger, aggression and acquisitiveness that are all too often aspects of our present age. Jesus' injunction to 'go into your room and shut the door and pray to your Father who is in secret; and your Father who sees in secret will reward you' (Mt 6:6) is an invitation to immunise ourselves against the increasing infiltration and impact of technology, travel and things in our time.

SECOND WEEK

SUNDAY

How can we fail to realise the need to stop this rat race and to recover the personal space needed to carry on a heartfelt dialogue with God? Finding that space may prove painful but it is always fruitful (GE, 29)

Luke begins his Gospel of the Transfiguration with the statement 'Jesus took with him Peter and John and James and went up the mountain to pray' (Lk 9:28). In the Bible the mountain is a meeting place where people encounter God. The mountain offers a space for what Francis calls 'heartfelt dialogue with God'. Thomas Merton, The American monk and writer, entitled his autobiography *The Seven Storey Mountain*. It related the journey he made geographically in grace to become a Catholic and Cistercian. He died in Thailand on a trip which took in the Himalayas and other mountain ranges. For him and many of his readers the mountain is more than a metaphor, acting as means of experiencing the mercy of God.

Luke often describes Jesus getting away to pray. This need for solitude is the nexus of his communing with God the Father. Today's Gospel celebrates a special event in Jesus' calendar of contemplation, the moment when his glory is manifested with his clothes shining 'like lightning'. Luke describes the delight of the disciples at being present and beholding the beauty of Jesus though Matthew also depicts their dread, adding the detail that Jesus touched them, telling them to get up off the ground and not to be afraid. The Transfiguration was a turning point in their travelling with Jesus as they followed him down the mountain, facing towards Jerusalem. This Second Sunday in Lent speaks to us of the need for 'personal space', the sacred spot where we allow God to touch us, telling us not to be fearful but faithful, free for our brothers and sisters, not fixated on our fantasies.

MONDAY

Do not be afraid of holiness (GE, 32)

Francis formulates a number of *Noli timere* – do not be afraid – sayings following on and flowing from the above affirmation. 'Do not be afraid to set your sights higher' (GE, 34) is not simply a call to heroism because it looks to the experience of God's love which leads to true human liberation. 'Do not be afraid to let yourself be guided by the Holy Spirit' (GE, 34) is not an abandonment of responsibility but a realisation that ultimately our human frailty and failure must lead us to where the grace of God can find us if we are to truly become free.

Without denying the reality of human shortcoming and sinfulness, holiness is a positive prospect. The pursuit of holiness does not rob persons of their 'energy, vitality or joy' (GE, 32). On the contrary, it enhances these qualities to a degree of excellence that exceeds human efforts. Holiness holds out the hope of becoming what 'the Father had in mind when he created you' (GE, 32). Francis declares that this is the dignity of the 'deepest self'. Like a seed lying in the ground, this self needs to be nurtured and brought to blossom through the co-operation of nature and grace. This is the holy self which is never hindered by the Holy Spirit but, on the contrary, is helped and even healed in the course of a person's life history. The search for truth, beauty and goodness in a person's life is an invitation not be fearful but a call to deeper faith, to trust that God takes nothing that is truly human from us. Growth in holiness always augments the greater good of the world and all who live within it. We need not be afraid of holiness because we are worth it in God's eyes and what the Father wants.

TUESDAY

Francis recognised the temptation to turn the Christian experience into a set of intellectual exercises that distance us from the freshness of the Gospel (GE, 46)

This reference to his namesake St Francis of Assisi comes in chapter two which deals with 'two false forms of holiness that can lead us astray' (GE, 35), the heresies of Gnosticism and Pelagianism. Francis devotes twelve paragraphs to the first of these, focussing on its contemporary features. Referring to an earlier description (in *Evangelii Gaudium*) he describes Gnosticism as the individual's interest in ideas and information which supposedly bring solace 'but which ultimately keep one imprisoned in his or her own thoughts and feelings' (EG, 94). Gnosticism is inimical to the Gospel because it isolates the individual in many ways. Firstly, it is an alienation from bodily existence, from simply being part of the world. Secondly, it involves an arrogance that assumes superiority over others through the stockpiling of a selected 'set of ideas and bits of information' (EG, 94). Thirdly, it is an abandonment of the Christian theological and spiritual tradition with its wisdom about the limitations of human reason and the sense of mystery that safeguards the transcendence of God.

With its denial of 'the deepest self', in which the individual finds their true identity before the living God, Gnosticism shows a disdain for encounter. Without encounter the Gospel cannot be undertaken, never mind understood. Gnosticism generates a fantasy which is foreign to Christian faith, building walls that block out the Spirit. Lent is a good time for taking stock of the temptation of a Gnostic tendency towards a lack of tolerance in our thinking. It is a time for asking whether there are particular preconceptions that we are fixated on, whether our hearts are so frozen that we cannot feel the 'freshness of the Gospel'. The figures of Francis of Assisi and Joseph (whose feast is celebrated today) serve as fine examples of saints who felt the freshness of the Gospel and followed in faith where they were led.

WEDNESDAY

Some Christians insist on taking another path, that of justification by their own efforts, the worship of the human will and their own abilities. The result is a self-centred and elitist complacency, bereft of true love (GE, 57)

A second substitute for holiness is Pelagianism. Instead of emphasising the intellect, this extols the will, taking pride in human activity and achievement as the answer to everything. This eliminates the grace of God, understood as the power of God to take hold of our hearts and transform us through conversion. The Pelagian attitude of absolute autonomy is always, to employ a phrase of Pope Francis used elsewhere, self-referential. At its base it is really a subjective stance, seeing nothing outside the self that can serve as an objective standard. In an age of increasing individualism and privatisation of people's lives Pelagianism has renewed appeal and presents a problem that can only be solved by a spiritual transformation of heart (and mind). Pelagianism points to the deep truth of the need for salvation which only God can achieve.

Francis identifies some new forms of Pelagianism among Christians. These include 'an obsession with the law, an absorption with social and political advantages, a punctilious concern for the Church's liturgy, doctrine and prestige' (GE, 57). An inordinate concern for 'self-help and personal fulfilment' is also listed here. This ecclesial egoism and elitism (which may extend to embrace others of a similar mindset) expends all its energy on satisfying this search for security, status and supposed sanctity, excluding evangelisation both of the self and others. In the concluding paragraph of chapter two Francis prays 'May the Lord set the Church free from these new forms of Gnosticism and Pelagianism that weigh her down and block her progress along the path to holiness' (GE, 62), encouraging 'everyone to reflect and discern before God whether they may be present in their lives' (GE, 62).

THURSDAY

Jesus explained with great simplicity what it means to be holy when he gave us the Beatitudes. The Beatitudes are like a Christian's identity card (GE, 63)

The Beatitudes are the basis of the Christian life so it is not surprising that Francis should focus on these in chapter three of *Gaudete*, entitled 'In the Light of the Master'. The lens through which we are invited to look is the person of Jesus for 'in the Beatitudes we find a portrait of the Master' (GE, 63). Conversion is the course through which Christians come to contemplate this portrait of Jesus and imitate him. Jesus has bestowed the Beatitudes to the Church as his spiritual and moral testament. In today's terms, the Beatitudes are the tweets that teach both the wisdom of holiness and the way of goodness.

Francis asserts that 'although Jesus' words may strike us as poetic, they clearly run counter to the way things are usually done in the world' (GE, 65). This poetic style is paradoxical, communicating that the Gospel often constitutes a counterbalance to the ways of the world. Described by some commentators as demanding the impossible, at least by human standards, Francis adds that growth in goodness and holiness through the Beatitudes can only come about 'if the Holy Spirit fills us with his power and frees us from our weakness, our selfishness, our complacency and our pride' (GE, 65). Lent offers a spiritual and liturgical space to look at each and all of these in our character and conduct. Recognising and seeking to remove them leaves room for the Beatitudes to take root in our lives so that we can become more (and more) recognisable as Christian. The Beatitudes are billboards of the heart that show what it is to both be and behave as a Christian, bearing the cross of Christ and bringing the fruits of his Spirit in the personal and communal mission entrusted on earth to us by the Father in heaven.

FRIDAY

Being poor of heart: that is holiness (GE, 70)

Francis looks first at the basis of security in life, whether we set our hearts on worldly wealth or on the word of God. He turns to the first Beatitude 'Blessed are the poor in spirit, for theirs is the kingdom of heaven'. Wealth will wear away and with it whatever we have, as Jesus' parable of the rich fool proclaims: 'he speaks of a man who was sure of himself, yet foolish' (Lk 12:16–21). This foolishness is at variance with faith which provides a foundation for both personal identity and involvement with other people through love. Being poor in spirit is a stance of openness to receive and offering in return, not closedness and covetousness. Inspired by his own background Francis identifies this state of spiritual poverty with Ignatian 'holy indifference'. This attitude, amalgamating abandonment and acceptance, is not very amenable to a culture that increasingly promotes acquisition, publicises arrogance and prizes ambition.

The Magnificat makes clear the choice and consequence between being poor or proud of heart. God strengthens the poor of heart while scattering 'the proud in the thoughts of their hearts' (Lk 1:51). Being poor of heart brings us the promise of holiness and happiness, while being proud of heart bears the prospect of hubris and unhappiness. In stark terms this is the contrast between spiritual life and death. Lent calls us to look seriously and sincerely into our hearts and consider whether we are allowing ourselves to be formed in the wisdom of poverty or the wantonness of pride. This will be reflected in the way we live and relate, in the lifestyle we follow. Being poor of heart is not a vague sense of spirituality but a vehicle for the values of the Gospel.

SATURDAY

Reacting with meekness and humility: that is holiness (GE, 74)

The odds that the meek will become masters of the earth seem long. Francis offers the insight on the third Beatitude that 'these are strong words in a world that from the beginning has been a place of conflict, disputes and enmity on all sides' (GE, 71). Thuggery rather than tenderness, terrorism rather than togetherness, toughness rather than taking care, this is all too often our world. To be blown and brushed away rather than blessed appears to be the fate of those who hold themselves humbly in life. Francis states that 'nonetheless, impossible as it may seem, Jesus proposes a different way of doing things: the way of meekness' (GE, 71). This is the way Jesus proposed to his followers, telling them to contemplate on and imitate his own gentleness and humility.

For Francis meekness is more than a moral virtue – a gift of the Holy Spirit which is active rather than passive. As a Gospel virtue it generates an attitude of acceptance of the frailty and even failure of others. Meekness means facing up to people and situations with a willingness to be thought of or treated as weak or even worthless. The meek may and most likely will not get their own way but that does not mean that their trials are wasted. Quoting scripture that even enemies should be treated 'with meekness', Francis is forceful in his assertion that 'in the Church we have often erred by not embracing this demand of God's word' (GE, 73). Responding with meekness rather than might, humility rather than hardness of heart is the Christian way. Lent asks us to look at this way of responding and repenting, realising that very often it offers the only real route to reconciliation in our relations with others.

THIRD WEEK

SUNDAY

We must first belong to God, offering ourselves to him who was there first, and entrusting to him our abilities, our efforts, our struggles against evil and our creativity, so that his free gift may grow and develop within us (GE, 56)

Francis often favours images from nature, using them to indicate the immensity of God's creation and the necessity of steady growth in response to God's invitation to flourish and bear fruit. This symbolism is deeply scriptural, drawing on the richness of Israel's experience of God and Jesus' employment of seeds, shrubs and other specimens in his expression of the kingdom of heaven on earth. Indeed Jesus' saying about the need for the seed to subside in the soil and die so as not to remain a single grain but supply a harvest is often interpreted as indicating his own sense of identity as the sacrificial Messiah who mediates salvation.

The parable in today's gospel for the Third Sunday of Lent points out a particular fig tree which has not produced fruit. The failure of expectation is felt in the frustration of the owner, formulated in his outburst to 'Cut it down: why should it be taking up the ground?' (Lk 13:7) However, the human calculus to cut one's losses yields to a compassion that consents to take care of the fig tree and give it another chance. In the past the prophets proclaimed that fallow land would become fruitful; in the Gospel of Luke the barren gave birth and the lost sheep was sought out and brought back to safety. The measure of God's mercy means that market forces, even in the garden, do not prevail in the long run. Survival is ultimately for the sake of salvation. Giving a second (and a third) chance is not a sign of weakness but of wisdom, 'so that his free gift may grow and develop within us'.

MONDAY

Knowing how to mourn with others: that is holiness (GE, 76)

Sadly, the faces of grieving parents and grandparents make an almost a nightly scene on the news these days. From chemical attacks to barrel bombs, school shootings to terrorist assaults on innocent civilians, the public mourning of those who have lost loved ones crosses all borders, the victims becoming household names. This public mourning moves many, even strangers, to share their sense of shock, suffering and sadness. Mourning features prominently in the Gospels too. From the wailing of mothers in the wake of the massacre of the innocents by Herod's forces after the birth of Jesus to the remnant, including his mother Mary, who remained at the foot of the cross of Christ, grief and the Gospel go hand in hand. Indeed, Jesus' ministry includes the moving scenes of his encounter with the widow at Nain and others who have been bereaved. The sight of Jesus weeping at the grave of Lazarus is the prelude to his shedding tears over the city of Jerusalem and the prospects of its citizens.

Francis states that 'the world has no desire to mourn' (GE, 75) with a lot of energy expended on trying to escape from the experience of privation and pain. Staying, standing with and supporting those who suffer the shock and sadness of being separated from family and friends after death is a making of the sign of the cross in the world. This solidarity, often shown in silence, is a sharing in the paschal mystery. 'Knowing how to mourn with others' enables people to 'embrace St Paul's exhortation: "Weep with those who weep"' (GE, 76). Mourning with others in the maelstrom of their misery ministers the mercy of God the Father of mercies, the compassion of Christ his Son and the consolation of the Holy Spirit. Mary, who knew both the joy of accepting to become mother of Christ to Jesus and the grief of bearing him at the foot of the cross, shows us how to mourn with others.

TUESDAY

Hungering and thirsting for righteousness: that is holiness (GE, 79)

Righteousness frequently carries the ring of *self-righteousness*, an aura of arrogance and superiority. Standing apart from others is an attitude that Francis has rejected again and again, in many forms and forums. Here he roots righteousness in the inner drives of hunger and thirst, relating the longing for justice to the basis of life itself. The need for justice is as essential as eating and drinking. It is the heart's requirement for happiness and as such is related to holiness. He states that the appetite for justice will not be satisfied by the 'daily politics of *quid pro quo*, where every-thing becomes business' (GE, 78). His rhetorical question about 'how many people suffer injustice, standing by powerlessly while others divvy up the good things of this life' (GE, 78) deserves to be repeated, even roared from the rooftops. A business as usual approach, with a mantra of you scratch my back and I'll scratch yours is the antithesis of the common good which is at the core of Catholic social yeaching.

Discipleship demands being drawn to and driven by 'Jesus [who] offers a justice other than that of the world' (GE, 78). Contemplation and imitation of Jesus in the Gospels inspires a passion for justice, implied in the interiority and intensity of hunger and thirst. The righteousness of God's kingdom is not a vague value and Francis warns that 'if we give the word too general a meaning, we forget that it is shown especially in justice towards those who are most vulnerable' (GE, 79). Lent asks us to listen again to the word of God and the teaching of the Church, to learn that enthusiasm for justice is not an optional extra for evangelisation. Encouragement for justice is best exemplified, for 'true justice comes about in people's lives when they themselves are just in their decisions' (GE, 79).

WEDNESDAY

Luke's Gospel is often given the title 'Gospel of Mercy' because mercy is the golden thread that runs through it. Sight is very significant in Luke's portrait of Jesus as the Messiah of mercy. In his encounter with the widow of Nain the evangelist expresses that 'when the Lord saw her, he had compassion for her' (Lk 7:13). Scholars say that this is a weak translation, the original meaning of the passage coming closer to a movement that comes from the depths of someone. His heart was literally moved with mercy at the sight of her mourning for her only son. In this miracle story Jesus raises the young man from the dead and gives him back to his grieving mother. Seeing and acting are two sides of the coin of compassion. Contemplation and imitation of Jesus call for conversion to this currency in our dealing with others.

Francis highlights another feature of mercy, that of forgiveness. He states that 'Jesus does not say, "Blessed are those who plot revenge"' (GE, 82) but calls blessed those who bear the hurt and do not become bitter because of it. In an interesting image Francis invites us 'to think of ourselves as an army of the forgiven' (GE, 82). An army of the forgiven will not face the foe and fight: its members are aware that all need and can receive mercy. The world needs this force more than ever in its history. Forgiveness is mercy freely given, without any terms and conditions. This is the measure of God's mercy, undeserved but unconditional. Unblocking hardness of heart, the celebration and reception of the Sacrament of Reconciliation is part of the process of repentance that Lent proposes. Conversion is short circuited if it cuts out the call to be reconciled to God and one another, to see ourselves as the recipients of the full measure of God's mercy and to treat others not combatively but compassionately.

THURSDAY

Keeping a heart free of all that tarnishes love: that is holiness (GE, 86)

In the sixth Beatitude Francis speaks of 'those whose hearts are simple, pure and undefiled, for a heart capable of love admits nothing that might harm, weaken or endanger love' (GE, 83). Heralding the hallmark of the heart as love, he proclaims that love protects the heart, promoting purity and pursuing perfection. He has written extensively elsewhere on love, especially in his profound exposition of the qualities of love proclaimed St Paul's Hymn to Love (1 Cor 13:4–7) in *Amoris Laetitia* (The Joy of Love). His initial comment there that 'the word "love" is commonly used and often misused' (AL, 89). Here he wants to avoid any abuse of love. This can only be achieved by linking love to truth. The Psalmist's line about God loving truth in the heart identifies the importance of integrating love and truth in personal identity.

In reminding readers that 'the Lord expects a commitment to our brothers and sisters that comes from the heart' (GE, 85) Francis is reiterating the centrality of conversion. The journey to purity of heart and perfection is primarily an interior one for 'from the heart's intentions come the desires and the deepest decisions that determine our actions' (GE, 85). Desires, decisions and deeds are the virtuous or vicious triangle that transform or threaten our own lives and the lives of others. Discerning our desires so that we can distinguish between what draws us towards or away from the demands of love is the litmus test for purity of heart. This discernment will determine whether our decisions will develop into deeds of love or their opposite, lust for pleasure, power and possessions that deface human dignity and destroy the hope of holiness. Keeping the heart 'free of all that tarnishes love' is the pathway to purity and the promise to see God.

FRIDAY

Sowing peace all around us: that is holiness (GE, 89)

Francis begins the seventh Beatitude by saying that it 'makes us think of the many endless situations of war in the world' (GE, 87). The word 'endless' makes things worse, if that is conceivable when considering conflicts that cause so much suffering. Pope Paul VI's address to the General Assembly of the United Nations in 1965 with his longing 'for war no longer' and passionate line that 'you cannot love with weapons in your hands' appears to have fallen on hard ground and harder hearts given the number of wars in the world since then. His successor on the chair of Peter continues the call of the Lord to put sword(s) back in scabbards and let modern day missiles rust in their silos.

Concerning the personal causes of conflict Francis considers that 'the world of gossip, inhabited by negative and destructive people' (GE, 87) does not contribute to concord between people and comments critically that 'such people are really the enemies of peace; in no way are they blessed' (GE, 87). The evangelisers of peace should follow the exhortation of God's word to work for and make peace, especially within communities when there is uncertainty about what is to be done. Peace protects and promotes community while conflict causes division and destruction. He admits that 'it is not easy to "make" this evangelical peace', that it is 'hard work' (GE, 89). With a strong note of realism he acknowledges that making this evangelical peace means not excluding but embracing 'even those who are a bit odd, troublesome or difficult, demanding, different, beaten down by life or simply uninterested' (GE, 89). At the same time this approach cannot afford to avoid conflict at all costs. In keeping with his earlier image of the army of the forgiven he asserts that 'we need to be artisans of peace, for building peace is a craft that demands serenity, creativity, sensitivity and skill' (GE, 89). How can we set about in Lent, personally and communally, acquiring these properties that make for peace?

SATURDAY

Accepting daily the path of the Gospel, even though it may cause us problems: that is holiness (GE, 94)

Francis begins the eighth Beatitude, 'Blessed are those who are persecuted for righteousness' sake, for theirs is the kingdom of heaven', by reminding us that 'Jesus himself warns us that the path he proposes goes against the flow' (GE, 90) and calls for a lifestyle that is the opposite of consumption, competition and celebrity offered as the route to happiness. Going with the Gospel against the grain of worldliness, wealth and war involves being a sign of contradiction. Trying to live by the Beatitudes will bring trials, being caricatured and ridiculed, even persecuted. However, martyrdom is the opposite of mediocrity and mediocrity is not an option for those who seriously take on board the Beatitudes. Gospel weakness is not being wishy-washy but a willingness to witness to the truth in love, even to lay down one's life. The wisdom of the word of God will not be wasted on waffle.

Walking the 'path of the Gospel' means that 'we cannot expect that everything will be easy, for the thirst for power and worldly interests often stands in our way' (GE, 91). On the contrary, those who genuinely attempt to live the Gospel can expect opposition in the form of indifference, insult and even injury. Holiness does not hope for hostility for, as Francis states, 'the saints are not odd or aloof, unbearable because of their vanity, negativity and bitterness' (GE, 93). It is precisely because of their humility that they experience the effects of vanity, negativity and bitterness emanating from the egoism and evil of others. Encountering hardship for the sake of the Gospel is the testing of gold in the furnace, the tasting of salt to see that it has not lost its flavour. Evangelical endurance earns the epithet of blessedness because, in the end, the kingdom of heaven belongs to 'those who are persecuted for righteousness' sake'.

FOURTH WEEK

SUNDAY

In a word [God] wants to give us a new heart (GE, 83)

One of the gospel readings for the Fourth Sunday of Lent has traditionally been titled 'The Parable of the Prodigal Son'. Some have changed this to 'The Parable of the Prodigal and his Brother'. The inclusion of the sibling is more than semantic, for it goes straight to the core of the parable, the heart converted to the Lord that is the source of compassion. This is the new heart that the Lenten journey directs us to, the draw of divine mercy that drives us to deal with others compassionately.

Writing that 'he came to his senses' Luke condenses the crisis that culminated in the younger son's change of heart. The direction of his life has led to the danger of his self-destruction. Repenting of the road he has taken, he responds to the instinct for survival and the invitation to salvation. Returning to his father's house he never gets to make public the confession contained in his heart as he is received with compassion and a celebration that exceeds his expectation or imagination. Even more than the Parable of the Prodigal Son this is the Parable of the Merciful Parent. The father is a figure of God who wants to give a new heart to both his children. Reaching out to the older brother he is greeted with a wave of resentment and reasons for rejecting the call to rejoice. Undeterred in his unconditional love for both, he replaces the acerbity of 'but for this son of yours' with the address 'My son' and appeal to accept 'your brother' (Lk 15:11–31). God's mercy embraces both the dissolute who have disobeyed and the dutiful who have become disappointed, the burnt out and the bitter. Lent asks us to look at the two brothers, seeing how both stand in need of salvation in the sight of God.

MONDAY

In the twenty-fifth chapter of Matthew's Gospel, Jesus expands on the Beatitude that calls the merciful blessed. If we seek the holiness pleasing to God's eyes, this text offers us one clear criterion on which we will be judged (GE, 95)

After quoting the line of Matthew's Gospel that indicates not only Jesus' involvement but identification in and with the hungry, thirsty, strange, naked, ill and imprisoned, Francis asserts that 'holiness is not about swooning in mystic rapture' (GE, 96). Rejecting images and interpretations of the saints seen as plaster or plastic figures with their faces turned fully away from any involvement with the world, he quotes Pope St John Paul II on the need to learn to see Jesus 'especially in the faces of those with whom he himself wished to be identified' (GE, 96). Thus the so-called 'Final Judgement' scene in Matthew's Gospel is not simply an invitation to be charitable but a call to conversion which continues to make present the mystery of the incarnate messiah. Contemplation of Christ is not iconic in the sense that it stops at looking on him but leads to seeing him in the poor and marginalised. We must not give into the inclination to simply gaze on Christ in isolation but give ourselves in imitation of 'the very heart of Christ, his deepest feelings and choices' (GE, 96).

He declares that it is his duty 'to ask Christians to acknowledge and accept these uncompromising demands of Jesus in a spirit of genuine openness' (GE, 97). He leaves no room for 'any "ifs or buts" that could lessen their force' (GE, 97). Rejecting relativism, Francis's call to action is intensified by the insight of fellow Jesuit Karl Rahner: 'Has there been sufficient reflection on the fact that, according to Jesus' speech on the judgement in Matthew 25, men [and women] are judged – it might be said 'atheistically' – solely in the light of their attitude to their neighbour?'[1]

---

1 Karl Rahner, 'The Church's Development Work' in *Concern for the Church Theological Investigations XX*, (*New York: Crossroad, 1986*), 67.

TUESDAY

There is the error of those Christians who separate these Gospel demands from their personal relationship with the Lord, from their interior union with him, from openness to his grace (GE, 100)

Sanctity and solidarity are not separate in the Christian vision. In the Old Testament the prophets proclaimed that faith and justice were constitutive of God's covenant. Sacrifice to God without support for the neighbour and stranger was not sufficient. In the New Testament Jesus proclaimed and made present the kingdom of God which St Paul described as 'righteousness and peace and joy in the Holy Spirit' (Rom 14:17). Paraphrasing the following line, the one who serves others in this way is worthy of God and has Christ's approval. The new commandment of love is the nexus of love of God and neighbour. This is 'the seamless garment' of contemplation and charity, dovetailing holiness and help.

He highlights the danger of Christianity (and the Church) becoming 'a sort of NGO stripped of the luminous mysticism so evident in the lives' of saints like Francis, Vincent de Paul and Teresa of Calcutta' (GE, 100). The Christian revelation and vision cannot countenance mysticism without mercy, contemplation without compassion, prayer without practise. The grace of the Gospel generates good works. As Francis notes, for these and other saints 'mental prayer, the love of God and the reading of the Gospel in no way detracted from their passionate and effective commitment to their neighbours; quite the opposite' (GE, 100). Faith and charity are not opposed, not either-or but both-and. Linking prayer and almsgiving Lent asks us to listen to the Scriptures, look at the lives of the saints, learn that action and adoration are not alien. Divorcing dedication to others from devotion does not do justice to faith.

WEDNESDAY

We cannot uphold an ideal of holiness that would ignore injustice in a world where some revel, spend with abandon and live only for the latest consumer goods, even as others look on from afar, living their entire lives in abject poverty (GE, 101)

Equally inimical to Christian holiness is any interpretation of the Gospel that sees it as bringing prosperity for the (chosen) few and poverty for the rest of society and humanity. With inequality increasing across all indices both nationally and internationally, Francis nails on the head any notion of suspecting 'the social engagement of others, seeing it as superficial, secular, materialist, communist or populist' (GE, 101). Christians and the Church must be engaged in the struggle for social justice which is not confined to interpersonal matters and relations but concerns the common good. Devoting several paragraphs to the theme of 'The worship most acceptable to God' he eschews any expression of prayer and devotion which eliminates encounter with others, especially the poor and the stranger. Devotion to God must dovetail with devoting 'ourselves to live generously, and allow God's gift, granted in prayer, to be shown in our concern for our brothers and sisters'.

He asserts that the acid test for the authenticity of adoration is to see to what degree it is converted into action, animated by the attitude of mercy. He quotes St Thomas Aquinas' statement that God has no need of our sacrifices but accepts them as a sign of sincerity and willingness to serve others. Holiness is not a haven for a privileged few who enjoy spiritual tax-breaks for faithfully saying their prayers while standing on the sidelines of the world. Sent as mirrors of mercy the saints show God's justice and truth, sharing in the struggle to transform the world for the whole of humanity. This is the only 'key to heaven'.

THURSDAY

We will find it hard to feel and show any real concern for those in need, unless we are able to cultivate a certain simplicity of life, resisting the feverish demands of a consumer society (GE, 108)

The seventeenth century French philosopher René Decartes, regarded as the founder of modern philosophy, is famous for coining the saying *Cogito, ergo sum*, I think, therefore I am. Today this rationalist motto is replaced by the marketing mantra, *Consumo, ergo sum*, I consume, therefore I am. While the deficiencies of Descartes' dualism have been well described down the centuries, the shift from thinking to things, being to having is without doubt most disturbing. Possessing rather than philosophising is the prominent and dominant mode of living for most people. Increasing inequality and lack of access to basic goods and services only highlight the crisis of a culture of having. Hailed as the hallmark of happiness, having more and more only leaves us, in Francis's line, 'impoverished and unsatisfied, anxious to have it all now' (GE, 108).

The consumer mentality not only devours things but also eats up time. Thus Francis states that 'when we allow ourselves to be caught up in superficial information, instant communication and virtual reality, we can waste precious time and become indifferent to the suffering flesh of our brothers and sisters' (GE, 108). Condemnation of a certain lifestyle is insufficient without the invitation to change. This involves a call to consider the course of our lives, to turning away from a preoccupation with things and possessions, to having time to take care of others and share ourselves with them in a spirit of solidarity, service and even sacrifice. This is the way of the Gospel which, in Francis's words, continues to offer all 'the promise of a different life, a healthier and happier life' (GE, 108), to which can be added a holier life.

FRIDAY

The signs I wish to highlight are not the sum total of a model of holiness, but they are five great expressions of love of God and neighbour that I consider of particular importance in the light of certain dangers and limitations present in today's culture (GE, 111)

Since the Second Vatican Council both Church teaching and theologians have spoken of the 'signs of the times'. This is an analytical approach that seeks to start from the state of the world, seeing and stating things as they are. This approach aims at arriving at a description of the general context, delineating good and bad situations, distinguishing light from darkness, depicting the draw(s) towards goodness and holiness or badness and evil. This helps to provide a picture of reality for people to engage in discernment, decision making and deeds. Before setting out 'a few signs or spiritual attitudes that, in my opinion, are necessary if we are to understand the way of life to which the Lord calls us' (GE, 110), Francis formulates those features that are the downside of daily existence, which drag people down, drawing them away from their deepest selves, dialogue with others and communion with the divine dimension of life.

These features are the faces of the human habitat of darkness. There 'we see a sense of anxiety, sometimes violent, that distracts and debilitates; negativity and sullenness; the self-content bred by consumerism; individualism; and all those forms of ersatz spirituality – having nothing to do with God – that dominate the current religious marketplace' (GE, 111). While Francis's focus is on divine mercy and not human misery, he feels it necessary to name these negative elements of human nature as they are expressed and experienced now. By looking honestly at the downside of today's world, we are led through Lent to avert our attention from what harms us towards what can make us truly happy and holy. This allows us to choose life over death, light over darkness, love over lust.

SATURDAY

The first of these great signs is solid grounding in the God who loves us and sustains us (GE, 112)

Grounding in God gives a person an absolute anchor in life, providing an invaluable place in which to encounter others and an indispensable perspective for engaging with reality. This interior space is the source of an individual's identity. This inner domain of dignity is indestructible despite what outrages and offenses may be directed against a person. Francis identifies this as the foundation 'of inner strength [which] enables us to persevere amid life's ups and downs, but also to endure hostility, betrayal and failings on the part of others' (GE, 112). Having this sense of self allows one to adopt attitudes of patience and constancy, adapting to life's changes, conflicts and crises. This deep-seated faith in God forms faithfulness to others, the loyalty which does not desert them 'in bad times' but accompanies 'them in their anxiety and distress' (GE, 112).

Being loved by God strengthens people to live by and speak the truth. This grace of God generates a meekness of heart that meets people without 'becoming carried away by the violence that is so much a part of life today' (GE, 116). A particularly virulent form of this violence is verbal carried by the vehicle(s) of social media. Such hostility may be shown in 'look[ing] down on others like heartless judges, lording it over them and always trying to teach them lessons' (GE, 117). The antidote to this aggressive spirit is humility which 'can only take root in the heart through humiliations' (GE, 118). Francis states straightforwardly that without such humiliations 'there is no humility or holiness' (GE, 118). The humiliations he is speaking of are the daily decisions to stay silent in certain situations, praise others rather than boasting about oneself, choosing 'the less welcome tasks' and 'even at times choosing to bear an injustice so as to offer it to the Lord' (GE, 119). Only those who are secure in spirit before God can contemplate imitating Christ in these sufferings.

FIFTH WEEK

SUNDAY

'Jesus' words are few and straightforward, yet practical and valid for everyone, for Christianity is meant above all to be put into practice' (GE, 109)

One of the gospel readings of Lent is fascinating as much for what Jesus does not say as for what he says. The story of the woman caught committing adultery (Jn 8:3–11), and dragged before Jesus does not mention her partner in crime. Whether due to a deep seated misogyny or a desire to trap Jesus, the scribes and Pharisees bring her alone before the crowd to face the wrath of God for violating the sixth commandment. Scholars and readers of the Gospel have long pondered about what Jesus wrote on the sand but the proverbial sands of time have long erased any trace of them. As this is the only Gospel that recounts this scene, the earlier story of Jesus' encounter with the Samaritan woman at the well and his pastoral attitude to her might be a suitable parallel for speculation about the words he wrote.

Despite the silence of the sands Jesus does speak three times. The first is to remind his audience, especially the scribes and Pharisees, that people in glasshouses should not throw stones. Secondly, after all her accusers and audience have slinked away, he simply asks her 'Woman, where are they?' This is similar in style and tone to his question for Mary Magdalene near the tomb after his resurrection. Thirdly, his refusal to reject her, 'I do not condemn you; go now and sin no more' is a reminder of the Evangelist's earlier line that 'Indeed, God did not send the Son into the world to condemn the world, but in order that the world might be saved through him' (Jn 3:17). This is the Gospel which grants Jesus the authority to tell the woman to go and give up sin. These 'few and straightforward' words apply to the scribes, Pharisees and others who also need to hear them as much, if not more so, than the woman.

MONDAY

Far from being timid, morose, acerbic or melancholy, or putting on a dreary face, the saints are joyful and full of good humour (GE, 122)

In his earlier Exhortation *Evangelii Gaudium* Francis exclaimed that 'an evangeliser must never look like someone who has just come back from a funeral!' (EG, 10) The exclamation mark exhorts Christians to exhibit a sense of enthusiasm in their encounters with others and everyday lives. Alongside mercy, joy is a major theme of Francis's pontificate, his persona, practise and proclamation combining to communicate that Christians need to look lively rather than deadly, reflecting the light of the Gospel. Tracing the thread of joy through the Scriptures he shows that this joy is not superficial but supernatural and 'brings deep security, serene hope and a spiritual fulfilment that the world cannot understand or appreciate' (GE, 125). The security, serenity and spirituality that he speaks of is rooted in rejoicing with the Risen Christ who promises his joy to the Church.

Christian joy is having a good humour. The saints are not sourpusses or stoics but people who are grateful for what they have been given and content with what they have. Referring to his namesake he states that 'Francis of Assisi lived by this' (GE, 127), gratitude for his daily bread even if it was hard and joyful in praise of God for the air he felt on his face. This joy of simplicity and simplicity of joy stand in marked contrast to the 'joy held out by today's individualist and consumerist culture … [which] only bloats the heart' (GE, 128). Indeed it could also be said to blind the mind with the barrage of marketing that is part and parcel of so many media platforms. Called in this Lenten season to discern the signs of joy or sadness, peace or anxiety, light or darkness in our experience, we are invited to continue our paschal journey with Christ to the glory of the resurrection so as to truly become evangelisers of Easter joy.

TUESDAY

Holiness is also parrhesia; it is boldness, an impulse to evangelise and to leave a mark in this world (GE, 129)

Francis devotes eleven paragraphs to this third feature of holiness. Based on the scriptural hallmark of boldness in the Holy Spirit it brings together both the courage and freedom of the Gospel. This is not the brashness found in so many areas and activities, ranging from advertising and business through media and sport. The only boasting that it offers is in the Lord, taking the lead from Jesus whose 'deep compassion reached out to others' (GE, 131), making 'him to go out actively to preach and to send others on a mission of healing and liberation' (GE, 131). The audacity that marks the Church is an antidote to arrogance, seeking to challenge the condition of the world and advance the coming of God's kingdom.

The need for boldness to bring us out of ourselves is especially great today with the emphasis on the self that can all too easily become egoism. Noting that 'like the prophet Jonah, we are constantly tempted to flee to a safe haven' (GE, 134). This harbour holds us back, imprisoning us in a spectrum of attitudes that include 'living in a little world, intransigence, the rejection of new ideas and approaches, dogmatism, nostalgia' (GE, 134). The Gospel galvanises us to burst through the boundaries we have established, encouraging us to encounter 'God [who] is eternal newness' (GE, 135). Evoking the image of God in Christ who, 'unafraid of the fringes himself became a fringe' (GE, 135), Francis exhorts us to be empowered by the energy of the Holy Spirit and embrace 'the example of all those priests, religious and laity' whose 'testimony reminds us that, more than bureaucrats and functionaries, the Church needs passionate missionaries, enthusiastic about sharing true life' (GE, 138). Following their example we can learn to 'stop trying to make our Christian life a museum of memories' (GE, 139). Christian courage constantly calls up and creates a horizon of hope.

WEDNESDAY

When we live apart from others, it is very difficult to fight against concupiscence, the snares and temptations of the devil and the selfishness of the world (GE, 140)

The cultural trend towards individualism incurs a tendency towards isolationism. When personal identity is interpreted solely in terms that the self creates and controls there is no room for community. Without roots in a community we may experience a sense of privation that is both social and spiritual. The African proverb 'one tree does not make a forest' proclaims the process and product of being part of something greater than oneself. Another proverb, 'a person is a person through other persons', indicates that relationality is at the heart of humanity and invites individuals to be responsible for the common good. Alongside a trend towards individualism in contemporary society there is a parallel proclamation of community, expressed in support for sports clubs and engagement with the local context.

For Francis, 'growth in holiness is a journey in community, side by side with others' (GE, 141). Alongside some tender examples from the lives of the saints, he emphasises the 'common life … [which] is made up of small everyday things' (GE, 143). Listing a number of 'little details' from the life of Jesus, such as the fact that one sheep was separated from the flock and the five loaves and two fish that he blessed to feed the multitude, he exhorts Christians to create communities whose members are cared for and where they may encounter consolation. Authentic conversion is a call to belong to that communion which is the true cradle of evangelisation. In imitation of the 'holy community formed by Jesus, Mary and Joseph, which reflected in an exemplary way the beauty of the Trinitarian communion' (GE, 143), the Church is a counter-witness to the ways of separation and selfishness, willing and working for the unity that Christ presented and prayed for.

THURSDAY

Though it may seem obvious we should remember that holiness consists in habitual openness to the transcendent, expressed in prayer and adoration (GE, 147)

In recent years there has been repeated emphasis on the role of virtue in personal and professional life. From business to sport, media to politics commentators and analysts have advocated a return to virtue as a remedy for the ethical crisis that has characterised many sectors of society. Virtues are character traits that govern and guide conduct in the dynamic of the drive to human goodness and the draw of divine grace. The key phrase in Francis's opening line on the need for 'constant prayer' is 'habitual openness'. This is the habit of openness to the horizon God holds out to humanity in Christ through the Holy Spirit. Thus Francis states that he does 'not believe in holiness without prayer, even though that prayer need not be lengthy or involve intense emotions' (GE, 147).

Luke's phrase about Jesus 'as was his custom' (Lk 4:16, 22:39) indicates the importance of the habit of prayer as the practise of opening oneself to God. Prayer becomes a habit. Quoting St John of the Cross about 'endeavour[ing] to remain always in the presence of God' (GE, 145) Francis emphasises the constancy of prayer which both creates and consolidates contemplation. Remembering that we are firstly and finally creatures called to become the children of the heavenly Father roots us in the habit of humility. Holiness is not a goal attained through human effort but a grace given by the mercy of God. Staying open to what God offers is the stance of those shown in the Scriptures who adopted an attitude of wanting, waiting for and welcoming the God who comes. Perhaps the patron saint of 'habitual openness' is Simeon who, 'in prayer and adoration' having awaited always the coming of the Lord's Messiah, welcomed his entry to the Temple as the child Jesus (Lk 2:25).

FRIDAY

In that silence, we can discern, in the light of the Spirit, the paths of holiness to which the Lord is calling us (GE, 150)

For Francis silence provides the spiritual space where our hearts are open to 'encountering God face to face, where all is peaceful and the quiet voice of the Lord can be heard' (GE, 149). It is impossible to imagine prayer without entering into silence at some stage, even and especially in the liturgy. Talk of encountering God in silence is not an escape from the world, a flight from others as if contact with them was somehow in competition with contemplation. Taking the image that prayer without silence is like the proverbial duck out of water allows us to think of silent prayer as the medium where we can be most ourselves and meet God most. Taking time and space to be in touch with our roots in the Holy Spirit enables us to grow and eventually reach out to others.

Francis insists that silent prayer is indispensable for discerning our personal vocation and path to holiness because 'otherwise, any decisions we make may only be window-dressing that, rather than exalting the Gospel in our lives, will mask or submerge it' (GE, 150). Prayer is not about adopting a posture where we can pass ourselves off, appealing to please God or appearing acceptable to others. Silence is the spiritual desert where we are stripped of superficialities, shedding our masks and seeking our true selves and paths. Jesus' call to 'put out into the deep water' (Lk 5:4) challenges us to move out of the comfort zone of correctness where we are in danger of drowning spiritually. Emphasising that 'it is essential for each disciple to spend time with the Master' (GE, 150), Francis exhorts us to embrace silence so that we can learn from Christ for 'unless we listen, all our words will be nothing but useless chatter' (GE, 150).

SATURDAY

Prayer of intercession has particular value, for it is an act of trust in God and, at the same time, an expression of love for our neighbour (GE, 154)

Francis rejects any interpretation of intercessory prayer as inferior. He has no time for what he calls a 'one-sided spirituality' which suggests that 'prayer should be unalloyed contemplation of God' (GE, 154) and which would consider concern for others as at best a distraction. For him intercessory prayer allows us to express 'fraternal concern for others, since we are able to embrace their lives, their deepest troubles and their loftiest dreams' (GE, 154). Adoring and asking are two inseparable aspects of Christian prayer, combining the commandments of love of God and neighbour. The vertical and horizontal dimensions of Christianity intersect in the prayer of intercession where addressing and asking God amalgamate. Trusting in God to take care of the needs of oneself and others brings together praise and petition.

This twofold pattern of praise and petition is presented in the prayer that belongs to all Christians, the Our Father. Professing the holiness of God's name is part and parcel of praying for the coming of God's reign and the doing of God's will. This triple   proclamation pours over into the three petitions for bread, forgiveness and deliverance. Christians can ask for these material and spiritual gifts for themselves and others because of their prior praise of God. God can grant these things because his holiness is not hidden in heaven but revealed in history. The Father knows that his hungry, sorrowful and sinful children stand in need of feeding, healing and salvation. Asking for these things is admitting and allowing God to act according to his mercy. Issuing from faith and incarnating love prayer of intercession identifies who God is. Faith and love flow into and out of each other continually, creating a horizon of hope.

 PALM SUNDAY

Some Christians spend their time and energy on these things, rather than letting themselves be led by the Spirit in the way of love, rather than being passionate about communicating the beauty and the joy of the Gospel and seeking out the lost among the immense crowds that thirst for Christ (GE, 57)

Today's commemoration of Jesus' entrance into Jerusalem offers Christians an invaluable opportunity for examination of conscience. In paragraph fifty-seven Francis contrasts two paths that Christians can take, forsaking or following Jesus as he journeys towards his passion and resurrection. The first path is pursued by those who parade the justification earned by their own efforts. This 'finds expression in a variety of apparently unconnected ways of thinking and acting' (GE, 57). Pursuing and promoting certainty and control, consumption and correctness, the people who are preoccupied with these concerns choose a path that is ultimately centred on self-aggrandisement and advertisement. This course of life is a refusal of the call to conversion.

The contrast with the path of Jesus' procession celebrated today could not be clearer. This is not a victory march where the winner takes all and is feted for worldly triumph, whether military or mercantile. Those who follow in Jesus' wake today and throughout Holy Week let 'themselves le led by the Spirit in the way of love'. Evangelical rather than egoistical, their energy is expended on passionately 'communicating the beauty and joy of the Gospel', seeking to evangelise and not be emperors of some earthly, even ecclesiastical, kingdom. Francis's line about 'the lost among the immense crowds that thirst for Christ' links today's liturgy with the ongoing merciful outreach of the Church's mission. As we enter into Holy Week we are asked to examine our consciences, to discern whether we are truly disciples of a Master who, as the humble messiah, 'is mounted on the colt of a donkey' (Jn 12:15).

Our path towards holiness is a constant battle. For this spiritual combat, we can count on the powerful weapons that the Lord has given us: faith-filled prayer, meditation on the word of God, the celebration of Mass, Eucharistic adoration, sacramental Reconciliation, works of charity, community life, missionary outreach (GE, 162)

In his introduction Francis stated that 'my modest goal is to re-propose the call to holiness in a practical way for our own time, with all its risks, challenges and opportunities' (GE, 2). He returns to this goal in the fifth and final chapter, 'Spiritual Combat, Vigilance and Discernment'. In a world whose history is characterised by so much conflict, much of which continues today, the theme of spiritual combat may not grab many headlines. However, Francis adduces another aspect of this struggle which may be both cause and effect: spiritual corruption. Corruption is front page news, involving individuals and institutions involved in almost every area of life. It is not sufficient to simply fulminate about such corruption, it needs to be fought against. For this reason Francis calls for constant vigilance, for 'if we become careless, the false promises of evil will easily seduce us' (GE, 162).

The spiritual and sacramental means of maintaining such vigilance and countering the corruption of soul are clearly listed. There is nothing novel in these, the tried and tested ways that through the centuries have helped holy men and women in all walks of life to do battle with evil, wary always of 'the wiles of the devil' (Eph 6:11). At the beginning of Holy Week it is good to be reminded of these 'powerful weapons that the Lord has given us' so that we can continue to rely on the help of the Holy Spirit in our hope-filled journey to holiness here on earth and in heaven.

TUESDAY

The gift of discernment has become all the more necessary today, since contemporary life offers immense possibilities for action and distraction, and the world presents all of them as valid and good. Without the wisdom of discernment, we can easily become prey to every passing trend (GE, 167)

Francis uses an example from the digital world to illustrate the variety of options for communication and consumption available to people today. A 'culture of zapping' creates a situation where 'we can navigate simultaneously on two or more screens and interact at the same time with two or three virtual scenarios' (GE, 167). This culture of zapping may not apply universally as of yet but it serves to indicate that there is a real danger of things replacing people, of our opting for objects over relations with others.

By alerting us to 'the immense possibilities for action and distraction' in contemporary culture Francis is acknowledging that is fundamentally an anthropological problem. The meaning of human life is increasingly measured by numbers, from hits achieved to what we have acquired materially. With morality interpreted in instrumental terms, individuals are itemised and indexed in terms of utility or its lack. This view of the human person is at variance with the vision of the Second Vatican Council in *Gaudium et Spes* which declared that 'endowed with wisdom, women and men are led through visible realities to those which are invisible' (GS, 15).

The exigency to discern the 'passing trends' of our times is echoed in the Council's prophetic pronouncement that 'our age, more than any of the past, needs such wisdom if all humanity's discoveries are to be ennobled through human effort' (GS, 15). In Holy Week we become even more aware that the 'wisdom of discernment' is arrived at through the sense of faith that sees the wisdom of the cross at work in our lives.

 **WEDNESDAY**

The devil does not need to possess us. He poisons us with the venom of hatred, desolation, envy and vice. When we let down our guard, he takes advantage of it to destroy our lives, our families and our communities (GE, 161)

Luke simply states that 'then Satan entered into Judas called Iscariot, who was one of the twelve' (Lk 22:3) while John declares that 'the devil had already put it into the heart of Judas son of Simon to betray him' (Jn 13:2). The moment of this betrayal is dramatically depicted in Caravaggio's *The Taking of Christ* which is on display in the National Gallery of Ireland. There is a mysterious irony in the title because Jesus gives himself totally into the betrayal of Judas. Caravaggio captures this contrast with his characteristic *chiaroscuro* style, the interplay of light and darkness indicating the battle between good and evil, the blessing of grace above greed, the boundary of life and death. The sadness of the scene, showing the moment when the intimacy between the Master and his disciple becomes infamy, is intensified by the straining movement of Judas to kiss Jesus in an act of recognition for those who have recruited him with a tawdry sum in silver.

Francis notes that the final word of Jesus in the Our Father, praying to deliver us from evil 'does not refer to evil in the abstract; a more exact translation would be "the evil one"' (GE, 161). Hence the evangelists refer to Satan/the devil. The tradition of *Tenebrae* on this evening when the candles are systematically blown out is a symbolic expression of how the devil can gradually lead us in a downward spiral of 'hatred, desolation, envy and vice' until we are completely dominated by the darkness of evil. On this vigil of the Sacred Triduum we renew our vigilance against the violence of the devil 'who assails us, asking daily for deliverance from him, lest his power prevail over us' (GE, 161).

 HOLY THURSDAY

Prayer, because it is nourished by the gift of God present and at work in our lives, must always be marked by remembrance. The memory of God's works is central to the experience of the covenant between God and his people (GE, 153)

The Evening Mass of the Lord's Supper celebrates 'the memory of God's works'. In the readings we remember the roots of our relations with God, beginning with the Exodus. Paul reminds the Christian community that Christ broke the bread and blessed the cup, telling those who belong to him, 'do this as a memorial of me'. Moving from Exodus to Eucharist, the Church is rooted in memory and renews in hope 'the experience of the covenant between God and his people'. The Gospel of the washing of the disciples' feet by Jesus reveals to us the reason for the covenant, the faithful love of God which we are called to remember by re-enacting in our service, especially of the poor and needy.

Francis encourages us to 'think back not only on God's revealed Word, but also on our own lives, the lives of others, and all that the Lord has done in his Church' (GE, 153). This gazing back gives rise to a 'grateful memory' which recalls and recounts the blessings bestowed by God. By retracing our journey and remembering our story in prayer we 'will find much mercy there'. This mindfulness of the Lord's presence and providence in our lives on Maundy Thursday moves us to remember that we have received so much in trust and renews our mandate to be missionaries in joy and gladness. Gathering in memory of and on the day when Christ communicated the mystery of his body and blood to the Church we go forward in faith, hope and love.

 **GOOD FRIDAY**

Whatever weariness and pain we may experience in living the commandment of love and following the way of justice, the cross remains the source of our growth and sanctification (GE, 92)

The Liturgy of the Word for today leads us to look on Jesus as prophet, priest and king. As a prophet he was passionate about justice, the righteousness which is part and parcel of the reign of God. Like his illustrious predecessors in the prophetic tradition of Israel he proclaimed that justice was integral to faith. Like Jeremiah and others he was prepared to suffer, even to lay down his life for his mission. Expecting our prophets to pronounce and protest even sometimes to the point of rage we are shocked by the silence of Jesus in his suffering where he shows himself to be a strange kind of prophet, even more unsettling than usual. The wisdom of Christ the prophet is not confined to words but communicated above all in weakness. As Paul reminded the Corinthians at the close of his second letter to them, 'he was crucified in weakness' (2 Cor 13:4).

The reading from Hebrews reminds us that Jesus is the supreme high priest who 'was bearing the faults of many and praying all the time for sinners'. As priest he is the prophet who prays his own self-offering once, for all and always. His sacrifice shows his openness to being 'obedient to the point of death – even death on a cross' (Phil 2:8). 'The mediator of a new covenant' he reveals that conversion is cruciform, calling into question all our concepts of God and casting doubt on our categories of correctness. Contemplating Jesus the crucified prophet and priest today we are called to bring our own weariness and weakness, willfulness and wickedness to the Father who communicates to us through the mystery and mercy of the compassionate Christ who will be crowned king. His 'eternal and universal kingdom' is composed of 'truth and life, holiness and grace, justice, love and peace' (*Preface for Christ the King*).

 HOLY SATURDAY

Enter into the Lord's heart, into his wounds, for that is the abode of divine mercy (GE, 151)

Holiness and imitation are often seen to go hand in hand. The theme of the imitation of Christ has been a staple of spiritual writing and has transferred to imitation of the virtues of particular saints, such as the poverty of Francis of Assisi or the patience of his namesake Francis de Sales, the little way of St Therese of the child Jesus, the sufferings and sacrifices of so many martyrs, named and unnamed. The inherent danger of describing imitation, even spiritually, is its dependence on ourselves, our decisions and deeds, even our dares. Holy Saturday invites us to delve deeper into the mystery of Christ, moving from imitation of him to identification with his weakness which involves immersion in his wounds. Having considered the works and words of Jesus in the course of his ministry we are called to contemplation of the cross and the tomb that contained the crucified Christ. Here conversion is not capitulation but surrender, compassion and not control.

Entering into the tomb we encounter the place where the Lord's pierced heart lay in death. Beholding his wounded feet and hands, we are brought beyond the hostility and hurt that the world and history hem us in with. Unlike the tomb that will be eternally empty after Easter, henceforth the heart of Jesus will always hold out hope for healing and holiness for 'that is the abode of divine mercy'. Immersed with Jesus in the tomb we learn through the wisdom of God that this is the womb of eternal life, the way where we exceed any notions of merit on our part and encounter the mercy which saves us and sets us free. This identity as partners in the paschal mystery produces the pattern of imitation that is the true pathway to holiness.

 EASTER SUNDAY

The New Zealand bishops rightly teach us that we are capable of loving with the Lord's unconditional love, because the risen Lord shares his powerful life with our fragile lives (GE, 18)

Love reveals the resurrection; the resurrection reveals love. Easter is our encounter with the love of God revealed in the resurrection of Jesus. This is eternal love, exceeding any earthly estimation or evaluation we can even imagine. Obedient to the Father's will in the offering of himself on the cross, the Father is faithful to his beloved Son, bringing him back from death and bestowing him upon the world as its Lord and Saviour forever. The love that goes between Father and Son gives us the Spirit, who generates the energy for us to become evangelisers and gathers us into the holiness of God.

The contrast between Christ's 'powerful life' and 'our fragile lives' is the cause of our Easter joy. The risen life of the Lord Jesus is not predicated on the political way of doing things in the world. His resurrection is not a prize and Jesus is not a victor in a winner-takes-all game. The resurrection is the noonday of the Good News, the Gospel of God's reign where power which possesses and oppresses is repudiated and replaced by the presence of 'the risen Lord' who remains with us to share, serve and save. This is the power of love, God's love and not some general principle that of goodness that guides life. As eternal Son and earthly brother the risen Jesus holds out the hope that that faith can fashion 'our fragile lives' into forms of holiness in the Spirit even here and now. Having immersed himself in our fragility, we can imitate his glory because, as Francis states, 'in the end, it is Christ who loves in us' (GE, 21). Easter reminds us that, today and every day, this is the reason to **REJOICE AND BE GLAD**.